AUDIO ACCESS INCLUDED

PLAYBACK+
eed • Pitch • Balance • Loop

T0088871

Audio arrangements by Peter Deneff

To access audio visit:
www.halleonard.com/mylibrary
Enter Code
4513-3816-6902-7559

Disney characters and artwork © Disney Enterprises, Inc.

ISBN 978-1-70516-362-7

Visit Hal Leonard Online at
www.halleonard.com

Contact us:
Hal Leonard
7777 West Bluemound Road
Milwaukee, WI 53213
Email: info@halleonard.com

In Europe, contact:
Hal Leonard Europe Limited
42 Wigmore Street
Marylebone, London, W1U 2RN
Email: info@halleonardeurope.com

In Australia, contact:
Hal Leonard Australia Pty. Ltd.
4 Lentara Court
Cheltenham, Victoria, 3192 Australia
Email: info@halleonard.com.au

ALL OF YOU

VIOLA

Music and Lyrics by
LIN-MANUEL MIRANDA

COLOMBIA, MI ENCANTO

VIOLA

Music and Lyrics by
LIN-MANUEL MIRANDA

THE FAMILY MADRIGAL

VIOLA

Music and Lyrics by
LIN-MANUEL MIRANDA

DOS ORUGUITAS

VIOLA

Music and Lyrics by
LIN-MANUEL MIRANDA

SURFACE PRESSURE

VIOLA

Music and Lyrics by
LIN-MANUEL MIRANDA

WAITING ON A MIRACLE

VIOLA

Music and Lyrics by
LIN-MANUEL MIRANDA

rit.

WE DON'T TALK ABOUT BRUNO

VIOLA

Music and Lyrics by
LIN-MANUEL MIRANDA

WHAT ELSE CAN I DO?

VIOLA

Music and Lyrics by
LIN-MANUEL MIRANDA